Amid These Empty Years

Brendan Tripp

ESCHATON™
BOOKS

http://EschatonBooks.com
978-1-57353-016-3

A LIGHT AS ACID AS BEFORE

Summation,
not caring, mists rise,
enter on worlds of cold and stone.

Vulgar nights tail sullen days,
virtue ruptures fabrics of conception,
all is madness, blind and vile.

Shells detach, days are peeled,
chaos opens as nightmares in the dawn.
Unknowing waker, your world does not come safe!

Desire seeds rejection,
hope births new pain,
a damning world is itself damned.

Cold hells,
flowed stone's entombments cast in fear,
a bleeding eye, the visage man's.

DUST FROM THIS SEEING

1
We sleep not waking
through many strata sleep
blind
slow
dragged down by tassels
bonds and know not why
2
In darkness dream
with no control
we lose the steerage
fade the helm
in daylight dreams
we reach for years
no gap retreats
no closer comes
3
I am the echo
from other wheres
I seed both dreams
with common forms
I am forgotten
on either shore
I claw night handless
all day alone
4
The waking call is too away
faint and dim
it rolls in whispers from the eye;
distraught, some phantom
yearns for this dawn
some knowing wraith
bleeds anguish locked
in somnolence,
yet too away
and too far gone
an echo of
no place no time
no being here
in waking sleep
no waking come
for vision

THESE PLANETS NOT MADE DAYS

Transferred insistence
in idiot missives,
lashed tight to the time,
held close to unknown.

I am not without,
I am not within,
scattered, disjointed,
things take new place,
strange new positions,
unsettling seats.

These, not the words,
this, not the face:
Armageddon comes knocking,
ribald and drunk,
confusion its fragrance,
digression our fate.

Vicious, these colors, on nerve ends too bright,
the sotto voice scream echoes through skulls
presumed to be filled yet ringing with space;
I fall, always falling, the empty and last.
　　No vista of vision,
　　no call in the night.

Attack:
One hand shatters the whole of the race,
one stroke breaks the crystal defining the wave.
Attack:
Crack the silence, pull focused the mind,
explode blackness in darkness,
wrench ink from no page.
　　Be all this inversion,
　　be madness and rage...

Defeat hovers languid,
existence is naught,
the void-clad masses convene and converge
lured by the feast, unknowing the meal.
Their steps, are they practiced,
are their passings rehearsed?
Are echoes not heeded from ancient agos?
Dust is their calling,
dawn lights up their trails,
sweeping and swirling without a new day.

AWAIT THE MADNESS OF THE DAY

These open and they dance,
painful, aching, dying souls,
wracked by true sanity,
order and greed.
Their sentence is the night,
it is their womb and prison,
the hollow chalice of their sweat.

Gyrate now in waves of heat,
dark streams of concept
wrap you and make you safe;
coil tight to illness, knowing pain,
embrace illusion and be its shades.

Noise to violence new shape has given;
whipped blood fountains, dark and rich,
spray the pulsing, aching air,
tear the world, destroy the setting,
shred apart the chain of man.
Silence echoes within this rage,
stillness harbors within the chaos.

Numbers run in moments' gaps,
forgetting rules the mind of night;
no form is left that holds to being
yet in its absence hangs still the web.
Bear up to pain, bear up to dawn,
the ersatz light will not you blind,
you of the vision, you child of night.
No simple order, no lying frame,
will take from you the ebon stain,
here badge and bullet, the sins of day,
cruel crystal sight among the blind.

ZEN VOODOO, BECOMING UNSEEN

Not what the horoscope
hasn't said,
nor what has not
been believed:
    It seems bad omens,
    strong juju,
    have turned ol' time
    upon its head.

Do not believe/do not
Believe
Can not see/can not
See
Never know/never
Know
    This comes a'calling,
    this comes to call.

You know its name,
its number's known;
its hour's appointed,
you've seen its ways...
    This is believing
    this is belief.
Pull tight the power,
pull close the strength,
nighttime's a ferment
deathly and dark,
filled full with reason,
purpose and cause.

No having,
no just:
    twilight twinkles, silver stars shine,
    blackness is calling, its tune is not far.
Not knowing,
not seen:
    rise from the coffin, spring up from the chair,
    float to the window, herald night's dawn.

ALL MEANING SLIPS AWAY

escaping words
held briefly, not in time,
not in sequence,
gone, order gone,
meaning gone,
lost words,
mind,
lost mind,
racing mind,
mind of moment, not of now,
slipped away,
mind of words,
words of thought,
thoughts of moment,
gone, gone, gone,
gone to where?
are they gone?

knowing not
we speak of toys,
fill with toys
a world of toys
not grasping time,
not filling time,
we make the order
not needing sequence,
place, or memory retreating
down channels fogged by days
and years of drink,
the missing drink,
the golden leash,
the muses' boy
lost without words,
locked up in time,
enslaved to mind
and hideous visions
of worlds of sober dying
dry scenes of broken sight

NOT THE PLACE NOR THE PROPER TIME

1
which way this way
which way that?

are memories proportioned
into simple cells,
monastic tombs,
lonely graves,
occasionally echoed,
called forth to haunt the mind?
are all pleasures doomed
to lie like this,
slight spectres nearly dead,
awaiting oblivion
in the dust of realer graves?

2
what years come down
to line an age?
what tumble of moments
creates tomorrow,
cradles today?

how to widen vision,
to stretch perception to vaster bounds?
the scope of man
is not enough to probe the truth,
to fathom the distance of total time,
how to break from human sight
to see as gods all things as one?

3
into darkness,
into the womb of night,
such comfort comes
why must to day
we be so enslaved?

FALL OPENS, SHATTERS, MAKES NEW GROUND

bang
something snaps in the world
a veil falls
the picture tube shatters

the movie looks all new

beginnings come in many ways;
a universe of doors,
open, shut, large and small,
flesh and freezing.
minds and metal

shards fall down
of splintered shells

like Christmas baubles hanging
within Christmas baubles, etc.,
each small breaking
reveals the world as much the same
but different colored,
with different warps and lines of stress

who is this newness now?

spanner, ringer, wrench, what all,
into the trudging gears,
into the spinning plot;
who writes in
the hairpin turn
in life's straightaway run?

it brings new context,
clear and cold

taught the legend,
time to grasp,
a door blown open in the blast,
falling through
new/old time,
not self or other,
not sure of where

LIMINAL LIFE, UNSTUCK IN TIME

What pictures rise
unclear, unsettled,
amid which words
will pictures rise?
Time returns to points of spreading
the days grow long and plans are set;
speak the number of the time
enumerate the day of death.

Not knowing, ride to pasts' enfolding,
in strange surround confront new names.
Take up the air of early autumn,
adjust your sight and catch these days.
Become not one,
not separated,
at thresholds stand
awaiting time.

Arise at center;
this is self, the sum sloughed off,
the song-read words from pages screaming
"new roads are hidden,
 unlisted ... find!"
Yet stasis holds a grip unyielding,
an acid grasp that kills in time;
and day drags on in useless seconds,
each set unwilling,
each lost behind.

IN SHATTERED DAYS

New modes addressed
on special days,
early days,
first of their kind;
strange places found familiar,
wrapped in haunting song,
shuffled in reason
and by distance ill defined.

These days come of being
yet uncelebrated stand;
only miles and difference hold their echoes,
alien in their colors,
unsettled in their ways,
as newly birthed on foreign plains.

Past the flow, in solitude,
drift with days and leafs alone;
new absence seeds again the sound
of days long gone and names that fade,
strange welling now
in cells of ancient stone.

Take off the fire that is here missing,
remove the cloak of wasted years,
erect new bastions against these days
that dwindle down to sorrow's baggage
and open doors for madness and decay.

Newness, wildness,
call this day,
they scream for needing,
their patterns,
charted paths that open fresh,
bear new standards,
new echoes of old truth.

Yet so unsettled,
so many things call of the age,
enslave the mind to things of day,
and slowly shatter
the shining crystal of our youth.

CATHEDRA PASSING, DAY BECOME OF NIGHT

Some days ring different
when struck by blows of action;
movement feels thicker,
more tactile and more real.
In the grasp of days like this
power runs raging through the soul,
dance is called to hidden drums,
sparks flare up from live cement,
and new names are answered
to questions of the self.

    It is not me
    this me
    it is not me
    not mine.

Desperate and dire,
tides are pulled as fingers twist,
shadows fly and darkness shudders
pulled away, unstuck from night.
New season blasts and rips the time,
shedding fragments, spinning violent to the void;
peeling mask from mask, self from soul,
frantic changes blurring focus,
overlaying and redoubling,
pulsing seething energies into hands
untrained and scarce aware.

    These take up
    this mantle, nameless,
    these take up
    this power and this see.

It is good and it is mine;
around me wrap all eddies of the day,
currents of the night,
insistent flows of riptide force,
swelling blindly, vast and newly born.
No name has this in time gone by,
no face deformed by this before;
I whip the fabric of space and time,
I shred the veil of mankind's world at last.
The day is coming,
this night has nearly passed.

ALL SPENT, ALL GONE, ALL WASTED LIFE

unsettled is the day
and from its chaos
poisoned is the week
and from its illness
broken is the month
and from its fracture
wasted is the year

this is the story,
the brutal truth

who returns from mists of time,
banished from the realm of sight?
this vision wordless haunts me now,
seeds thoughts of pleasure,
an itch insane

defray these costs,
defer the time of last account,
this side is sheltered
but threatened by the wake;
I have not data
but only fear
entrapment and enraptured states

they multiply, these names,
they so expand to break the mind,
no simple self in single thrall
but spilling masses
engulfing time

no saga this,
no hero's tale we tell

chaotic is the day
in chains unsettled
ill is the week
in poisoned bondage
fractured is the month
in broken spirit
wasted is the year
which seeds the waste of life

NOT SET WITHIN ONE TIME

obscure
and bad dreams waking
shot by night,
ripped ragged
by the slow decay
timed subtle, twisted,
cellular intrusions
wracking nerves
and handling thought
unwell

> be of this being
> you who are lost
> be of this vision,
> this vacuum, this pain

not sure
discussion rages
wild in silence,
warring tides
pull each their way,
taped patterns play
long past their being
long into new season
the singings of death
unheard

> take down and open
> skulls for their data,
> take down and scatter
> the lines of this place

secure
in settled highways
free of ruts, cast in stone
ossified vector sightings
not heaven taken
too brutal breaths
inverted, reversed,
torn back, revealing
sightless, mindless,
undead

> fly in fleeing the night
> locked ever in its cage.
> fly in fleeing the day
> to shores unknown be taken

THE FIRES OF THE DAY

1
This is hell,
surely this is hell,
no sulphurous fumes or charring flames
could be much worse than this burning,
this ringing, this pounding in my head!
Damned world,
damned race,
I hate you all and all of you;
I can not breathe but feel this rage
I can not feel except feel hate!
Let me alone,
let me away,
allow me sleep that ends not in pain,
allow me waking that burns not with rage;
allow me calm, or death, or void,
let all this end, all this destroy!

2
Through days as dark as night
and nights insane as day
I, we, hurdle blindly, stupidly,
lacking vision, without plan.
Sometimes there is no god, no devil, and no right,
> and churches burn
> with fires of earth,
> earthly hells denied by heaven,
> cast down in hatred,
> despised by their creator
> who is absent, nonexistent,
> missing, missed, and miserable.
Sometimes mind itself is damned,
hated, and wished towards death;
accursed intelligence that makes us see
> the lie of living,
> the idiots we all must be,
> locked stupid in an unset world,
> seeking patterns
> in the eternal maddened shift.

3
Become this now in rage of being;
no chemical salve will save the night,
no comfort come of blind believing,
no soothing morn will greet our sight.
> As all is lost,
> all damned,
> and all decayed.

Rise up as madness, all insane,
make now this chaos
a fitting cauldron for all our hate,
a crucible for our destruction!

4
Dark hanging, sick air,
unwholesome place, black as the grave;
we are all locked, chained in this charnel,
doomed to a bone-pyre but never set free.
Pus is our water,
feces our food,
light pours down acid,
destroying our sight;
unceasing come calls of dying and death
in our voice and others
but never at rest.
Freedom, what's freedom?
The world is our cage,
we are damned here, despised here,
and sentenced to die
unpitied, unmourned, weakened and bent,
broken of spirit and ground to the dust.
There is no escaping,
there is no release,
no solace in fictions of joy, love, or care;
no freedom but death,
embracing the night.

5
Take fire,
take rage,
bend all things to hate;
seed Armageddon with chaos and death,
water its growth with blood in the streets,
herald its coming with explosive desire!
The world is damnation,
the world holds us slaves;
tear down all its order,
erupt with despite,
shatter and smash its puling facade,
crush insipidity, comfort, and hope,
seed terror and madness,
the whole thing destroy!
There is no real goodness
in this damnable world,
no truth, no pure beauty,
no permanent joy;
destroy it, remove it, tumble it down,
cremate creation, hell's blackness ignite,
wipe clean the cosmos of pitiful life!

THIS AMERICAN RAGE

hating the world,
enraged at mankind;
wishing to burn life strangely,
burn life darkly,
burn life quickly
and snuff out,
to run the way of my own damnation
and let this world go damn itself,
and all to die ...

yet hate
and all this burning makes me live,
makes me strive,
makes me keep on dying in existence
built of anger,
built of rage,
keep on being so unwanted,
so damned, banished, and exiled,
so full of hate ...

I dream of killing,
I dream of raging and of dread;
I sleep in maelstroms of anger, dread and blame,
where peace and joy and love are lies,
happiness a stupor built of drugs,
drugs and liquors I'm denied,
in this damned world,
in this real hell,
in this stinking pit of all mankind

AND WHEN SHALL THE CROWD AWAKE?

by this hand taken
by this hand made
in these words echoed
all the action of the past

by losing self
to current day
by slaying thus
the face of man
another world awakes,
     clear, clean, familiar
     near as night
     built of shadows,
     dreams and fears

mad is this world
and all its people
mad
and of this madness
might we build
a stranger slant to life
asylum house
loose in the streets
not pretending to be sane

afeared and lonesome
are they all
locked to seemings
and propriety's steel grip
how better life
to be set free
of mind and reason
thought and pride
free from dreaming
the lie of mankind's sleep

by these hands taken
by these hands made
in words here spoken
we erase of all our past

EUTHANASIA. DEATH'S COLD HAND

too much here,
just too much here,
too much of strain,
too much of stress,
too many things
demanding time
and birthing panic,
madness spawned of fear

between extremes
the soul is torn,
from raging terror
to saddened signing blues;
no good, no light,
no happiness comes here
each thought, each word,
a brick troweled on
to this entombing wall

sick, so sick,
deathly ill by day and night,
slow death is here,
slow poison heaped
by word and deed and attitude
swirled deep around
in deadly air,
in atmospheres diseased;
the gallows this,
a place of death indeed

march on with time,
march to cold hands,
ice grip of death,
the reaper's cruel embrace;
seek out sweet sleep,
kind blankness find
in mindless void
and selfless black,
fade off in dying
from living's pain

TEN THOUSAND THINGS FOR THE JUGGLER'S ACT

and up,
and up,
spheres of distaste
spheres of need
spheres of demand
spheres of desire
spheres of want
spheres of should
a thousand spheres
up in the air
a thousand items
for juggling time,
up, catch, up,
no time to catch up,
up, and catch,
up, and up,
all must fly
all must be
attended to
and all at once
each sphere a glimmering
globe-like world
each bearing being,
desire, demands,
priorities and other scales
that pull emotions
this way and that,
that dictate the place
the universe is
for that fleeting moment
it rests in the hand
before it goes up
back into the air
before it's transposed
for the next gleaming sphere
and the next world of being
and the next place to be
and the next way of thinking
and the next side of me
and up, catch,
and up,
and up, catch,
and up

DIVIDED COMING OF THE DAY

1
not taken up:
broken night's wail unnoticed
2
blackness hinged
leaves hints of white
tales of distance
and sad day
   3
   becoming now,
   the doctrine of the age
4
all these leave
traces on the skin
all these write
histories
5
from this
from this
all process seeds from this
echoed long from bitter night
the yarns of terror
the epic breadth of being
6
divide the hour
divide the day
homecoming breaks,
falls shattered on the grass
   7
   grave seasons come
   in apertures too wide
8
defused.
breath holds frozen
too solid to have flown,
too ephemeral to fall
9
these reasons echo,
equivalence reverberates,
erupting blooms too soon from seed
and rips sky bloodied
no longer full of ruptured time
10
begone besides
became bemused
because

NO BALM TO HEAL THE POISONED SOUL

each day
brings new theaters
for isolation's play,
each action
new fuel
for dread and distance,
anguish, pain, and hate

I lose track,
drop threads,
am blocked from context,
dropped from life:
each instant runs eternally
while hours slip to moments,
thoughts once cogent
now seem befuddled,
robbed of line;
planning is impossible
divorced as this from time

and help,
when offered,
is really curtained hurt,
blind actions focus
way too sharp
and slash in darkness
at my soul
dividing up all of my care
destroying corners,
last vestige of the safe

the fools,
the fools,
they blindly slay me
yet make me live
in living blackness fed by rage
by illness reaching to the soul
by death corroding all insides
to hollow void, no heart, no soul

this is their hand,
my hand, all bound
together in this pointless dance
for I am ill and they are blind
and all is death,
dusty and decayed

UNSET, UNSETTLED WITH THE NIGHT

1
where has mind,
continuity flown?

what place is this?

2
the numbers become
too small
and spread retreats
to insularity
    this too pulls in
    this too draws close

I soon suspect
these walls will kill

3
fading, fading,
illness, faint,
absence wraps its tendrils round my soul
and draws the self away

how thin the thread

4
why are these special,
these grieving eyes,
that only they
might see these chains,
and see the waste
of fleeting life?
    too soon do schedules come
    too real are deadlines' lines

it is here
that sadness lies

5
because the reasons
all must fly
and nighttime leave
entwined with day

because of this

DENIED THE PAST, WITHOUT A NAME

again the symboled voice
comes up short,
struck abrupt
against the tide of words
that are the same,
that only shift,
that form the chant
droned long on
while echoing a sort of sleep

where does the vision go?

in this we see
a view within,
locked patterns sing
a song of days
spent as the dead
or even worse

the chasm is both deep and wide
rotted, yes, but not quite dry,
not powdered to some simple dust
but foully stinking, damp with rot,
held up by seething bands of fire;
nice day in here,
nice place to die

I seek to say
these things with blanks,
but holes fill up the total screen
and spin a vortex deep to doubt:
it's all the same,
same world, same place,
held hollow, ill, and like to death,
no home this is,
no place to stay,
where nothing enters from without
but themes of madness, rage, and pain,
made poignant by assuming hate
and making all
apart from me

where goes this life,
fell absent,
down the drain ...

DARKNESS FROM THE NIGHT,
BLACKNESS FROM THE SOUL

1
deep blackness
and outer void
vastness stretches
beyond vocabulary,
hugeness stretches
beyond the mind

scale collapses,
concerns deflate,
reason is frozen,
impaled by immensity
too great to touch,
too awesome to approach

> words seek to wrap
> around this silence
> but gape and stutter
> at lack of ends

2
beyond the event horizon
the singularity waits,
mass crushed out of space,
driven out a point
dragging time
and space and light
to what, to where,
leaving draining pulls
irresistible in its wake

beyond the furthest star
the outer film still flees
further, farther out,
but out to what, to where,
beyond the surface of the all
streaking off from central fire
condensing darkly on the fly
to freeze in silence or rebound,
return to flames anew,
a final flash of dying

3
so hollow seem
these movements here,
so tiny seem these hands
and all the works of hands
like them,
so useless and so weak,
built in blindness, ignorance,
insect frenzy

sad race,
dragged up from slime
to see the stars,
you fantasize that
somehow it matters
to the reeling trillion,
trillion. trillion stars
that each life comes
and each life goes,
and all your bricks
and tears and sons,
might have some point
amid the spreading dark

4
when seen by light
of galaxies tasting death
all faith seems shallow,
anthropomorphic screaming
done in whispers in stone caverns
hunched down low to hide from void
dark beyond your eyes so blind

NOT MILES INTO ETERNAL SPACE

during the days of madness
fear trembles rampant
conjuring the unknown,
hate makes all reason
falling, fade away,
down, hidden,
enfolded in some shuffled crease
in some corner, room,
forgot, distant in both space and time

fleeing fails
absence tumbles, not enough
to make the break
with darker selves
although in chanting seek to die,
seek to juxtapose and shatter
this from that,
presence with away,
ending with freedom, held beyond my grasp

disturbed and missing,
wrapped with words spit out in rage,
in dissention against this life,
and tunes too happy for the tale
hanging hours long beyond their time;
are these echoes
of shots fired silent in some fight
yet undeclared but new a-flame
made understanding, revolution, war?

all is dark but new informed
of details, problems,
plans not yet made
    almost of flight,
    broken cords that bleed their hate,
    run to fictions of far away
    ungelled in mind beyond one day
    not stretched to futures,
    not miles into eternal space
torn down to basics,
to rubble, dust,
and still the same long ride to void,
long sweep of moments lost to our lives,
lost into sorrow, memory, regret

SWUNG SLOWLY BY ILL WINDS

1
anguished dead puppies
made violent by the night

2
absenting within,
without;
disrupted sight bleeds in chorus

3
desired song
in missing mirrors,
unnamed years
pass into indistinction

4
it costs too much to be this me,
it tallies up the curse of days

5
new schemes unfold
in unsure blooms
made poignant by these dying ways

6
act all these lines
and so decide,
a spanning will
takes all the pins

7
greatness leaves traces
long nights into the dark

8
return, return,
pattern etches,
makes brutal ruts the norm

9
a scream upsets the even course,
bloody scream from deep within:
this soul is fading,
bringing ebbing to the corpse

SHOOK MADDENED RUN BY DAY

because of reasonings
held rancid, rambled,
brought forth from time
divorced from truth
    where is the tape?
    where is the record?
    flight comes to being
    and echoes no trace
blocked down, encumbered,
fingers run too slow for mind,
they need a voice, some way to call
to bridge the gap and not go back
to seed the page with unheld vision
all tumbled out against the white
    I would sleep become,
    I would distance
    far and easy
    thick and grey
almost panic's sweep in channels
swelling sight of past agos
unseasoned day, unseasoned time
in nights too hot the sweat filled cauldron
a-brim with movement, action, life
    decay down from this moment
    break off the stiff facade
    dissolved to chaos
    enumerated the final days
breathing heavy, breathing hard
pain shoots out to fill the eye
that turns within to only know
the solitude that spans the night
the blackest age of failure felt
until the dawn, until new dawn
    unbiased rite of unwicked flame
    and crystal altars' shine
    unsullied here so far away
    so distant set beyond the mind
driving passion driving day,
a world set fire across the globe
by scheduled hours, untempered pain;
brutal, evil, unwholesome life
froze to iceage, locked to stone
made like death, like dry and bone

IN VISUAL CHAOTIC RAGE

come into chaos
without limiter or control
they echo other's words
older words brought in again
from exile into penalty,
vision into sight;
these are the denizens
of deep jungles of despair,
maddened and sweating,
making calls of agonies
unseen, well hid
amid the twisting brush

thoughts built of place,
plane, erupt in minds
too addled for a plan,
ideas flash and bounce,
careen around the mental gym
like BBs spraying,
like subatomic virtual birth
made concrete, symbolic,
realer than the real;
these seek a place in outer worlds,
seek for harbor,
recognition and some sight
that brings wide vista
like that of other pens

but crash, decay
inflicts again the world
upon intent, hope,
envelops all in thick despair,
molasses apathy too slow
to make a worth of any act
seen shadowed in the mist;
how sick are days built of this stuff,
how brutal time chained to its weight,
this leads to waiting long on death
and prayers for mad chaotic realms
that reach beyond the mental sphere
to burst all bloody on the world
and make a balance with withins
    these are the ways
    of this dark crypt,
        cocooning stone
        entrapping life

A JOURNEY TURNED TO SLOW

white hair hangs sadly,
harbinger of age,
plucked away from unwilling flesh
not wanting to tote up the years
placed on mirrors, as windowed time
remembered none the less

    whole flocks of birds
    have taken flight,
    from valley forests rise
    like darkened clouds
    up to the sky
    and so away,
    they fly away,
    recede in distance never spanned
    forever off they fly to where
    no echo may return

so comes turning
of the age,
a meter click
against the fare of time
held ransom, silent,
known to none
but cabbies cloaked in dark
that steer unheeding
our plaintive yells
"turn here", "go there",
"please pause here for a while",
they know the route,
when it is done
the station is the same

    dawn cuts slowly through the mists
    that taunt this dusty plain
    wind whips hair about the bones
    of lifelessness in life

it is the pit
at which we stand
swaying nauseous at the brink
portals open,
walls define
the passages towards death
held open, waiting,
bleeding time

ACCURSED AND FADING FROM THIS LIFE

no good is
but decays;
no hope bears
joy in its fruition,
only anguish,
dissolution born of shattered dreams,
the fantasies of what might be,
always lies,
always fictions
broken down on what is real

and what is real
is pain,
is sickness,
is feeling so betrayed by life
and by all those who spread the lies
of joy, of love,
of happiness,
perpetuating illusions
of what can never be

within this life I crave for death,
yearn for states not built on lies,
seek the freedom of the grave
which is the one true state of man;
for living is but vileness here
beyond all love,
denied all care,
trapped in this place of no escape,
no relief,
amid the shards of shattered hopes,
rotted dreams ground by the heels
of oppressive truth,
the putrid real

it all sinks lower
every day,
like metal plates in endless seas,
lower, colder, deeper still,
seeking out some darkest place
at which to rest,
to hide,
entombed beneath the crushing mass
of all that passed on its way down,
damned by the weight of history,
cursed by the very state of life

TO DIE FROM HERE, TO GET AWAY

1
it is the falling of time,
the crumbling of blood and sweat
to new modes of decay
brought low and saddened,
crushed beyond all recognition

2
all beauty
implies decay,
all attraction
implies rejection;
    implications
    become real,
    emotion springs
    from its perception

3
drop down,
hug floor, cement,
lick tile;
world too big,
too full of hate,
drop down to hide,
perchance to die

4
there is no growth,
no line connecting,
just the rot of rife return;
it eats at mind,
it shuffles breathing,
it stinks and will allow no good

5
pressures strain
on metal wires,
sinews tighten
against the pain,
    apart we wait
    and pray for breakage
when shearing comes
there will be violence,
when being snaps
there'll be escape

LOST INTO THE WEST

decay ensues in absence
as days through fingers slip;
concentration
will not congeal,
not form around the sinking mind
here wallowed and confused,
made muddled by the breadth of pain
encountered in the world

no where, no when
is crystal form uptaken
and honed to brightness past the day
in hardened shine,
keen excellence,
the cutting edge of perfect souls
made hallowed by pure mind;
no, this denied,
in this failed
the heart breaks down and blubbers

each turn uncovers
more disease,
more rejection, deeper scorn;
each visage crumbles into shards
that pool and melt,
coagulate
so to reveal the truer face,
the crueler side,
the darker harbor of my night
more hideous than even dreams

> no validating
> is found herewith,
> not from the right or leftmost sides
> sought out in panic,
> escape and fear

cycles are still set to turn
as is their wont
and sole demand,
but place seems shifted to the ill
as though set down on unwise squares
or dying paths;
this seems
the hatching of the end,
the chapter of the sunset ride

UNSURE OF CORNERS, ADRIFT THROUGH PLANES

place extended through the haze
unsure,
unsettled,
made floating by its doubt
carried softly through the spheres,
all one question,
united as why
with overtones of what and who
in wheres and whens
too shifty to define

books we read,
random pages filled with lines,
that beg some contest,
some comparison with marks of day
made halting in the ebon light
unguided,
not the same,
unlashed from anchors to their world
as though the eyes
were plucked from out the head
and blindness staggered
unknowing into day

the sun erupts across the streets
with waves of heat and glare
yet these come filtered,
kicked out of line,
arriving more as symbols, charms,
shorthand forms for what they are
and never quite the thing itself
never stripped,
never bare,
never naked in perception's arms
caught sweaty for the empty page

the mind runs down
and empties soul's cup of despair
now drunk with sorrow,
blind with the draught of doubt,
it stumbles, searches,
fights the panic of locale
so unaligned. devoid of place,
bereft of guideposts of the way,
all lost to tides,
the drifting currents of dark time

LATE, PUSHED AWAY

these fantasies
fade, shift within
the night
plans show the fool
again the fool
and underline
the uselessness of life

all hope breaks down
shatters on rocks
as love denied entwines with hate
despising and regret
made hollow with each breath
took with no point,
no reason

the hours slip
and flee away
the dual urge hangs with us
as it so often does
in late nights torn between no sleep
and dreaming sleep
forever taken as escape

the passing comes
into the darkness
enfolding to scenes afar
yet this is falling
and not escape
surrender
devoid of flight

AT THE RESTING OF THE SUN

1

walk in strange surrounds
take hints of flora nameless from the air
find isolation shaded by unnatural streams
and the markers of the great now gone;
run, hide from the incursion of the race
attempt the heights attacking at the legs
and settle for the rocky perch
more easily attained

2

place unfolds ill-defined,
strides tick off too slow
against the background distance scaled
too wide, too high
too much to fit the simple eye;
the clock races
as dust lifts and sweat begins to bleed,
what illusionist
creates a place like this?

3

breaks form,
cracks intrude throughout the night
denied the slide to black;
these dealing numbers of the air
prevent the taking of retreat
and fill the pages line by line
with active verbs
not run with dreams

4

gears of being mesh in time
and cross location with morning's doubt
unsure, displaced,
cut adrift against the flow of life
not settled nor allowed respite
days tunnel future paths
without consulting human plans

AVID AVERSIONS TO AVER

too full,
arrives unsettled
with not enough numbers
to call for hiding
deep within some blanket form
of cheap discussion
reminiscence of the ways
now parted back
slipped into time

    a pause becomes a whip to time
    against the passage
    deciding when and how a flow
    defines a place, a two head zipper,
    a fleeting window too hard to mark
    and wonder where
    the midpoint enters
    when lights the light
    that says "half there"

    unlike these souls
    for man is easy
    each final breath totes up one more
    another stiff
    another past tense on a name
    just one more standing
    on the majority's side
    of the slippery line
    the tenuous thread

but there again
the tides internal wrench
strange things with clocks ring the mind
and echo down the empty soul
each point brings pressure
each vector promises decay
no path leads off beyond this focus
so numberless
locked up again
rewrapped in chain and not away

DUSK HANGS A SECRET FOR THE AGE

1
Strange meshing,
twisting threads from different times
involving here,
unfolding here,
expressing here new ways of sight
that cut through clouding
brace the mind
with crystal structure newly clear
unhook the soul
from places stuck
and spin new ways
to purify.

2
I walk into this sea
too warm, too soft,
too strange a water to be known
    whose hidden depths
    mask ancient lands
    millennia unseen.
I float amid the saline wash
and drift with memory,
waves and wind,
returning back to long agos
so soft, so warm,
so like before in ocean dreams
    as firsts return
    but out of place
    now long gone on.

3
Growth,
can this be seeded here,
can new paths open,
options spring,
from mere handfulls of day?
    The body aches
    and screams for control,
    its pains and lusts insatiably clamor
    to be the center,
    to strip away the thin veneer
    of concentration on true needs;
    the mind battles confusion,
    the heart finds yet new depths.
Is this the cauldron
for new age,
the oven baking
sweets for time?

ONE PLACE UNTOUCHED

the exile roams nights
and streets not warmed
by summer sun
in search of food
in search of solitude
these journeys made alone,
always alone,
wrapped in cloaks of isolation
huddled deep against the race
vaguely fearing
gut set against contact
strange and unsettling
layered in dread

history's weavings
leave traces of pain
piercing the mind,
threading the heart;
the trails lead through darkness
and sparkle color through black
causing dull recollection
to flare in the brain,
red flashing to yellow,
hurt lashing to rage,
they drag down the soul
far into the past
and make it a stranger to day

something of night
brings comfort,
something of darkness
gives promise of hope
against the ravages of day
so central, so steely,
so like the stone walled cage
of this entrapment;
the city embraces
and coddles its own,
it makes cement yield in ways not yet seen
and offers its secrets as gifts to the child
left stranded in its massive care

BY SORROW'S SOUND BEWAILED

1
it begins to sputter
it begins to die

turnings pulled in
retracing old steps
cut ruts too deep
that seek to break
issue darkness,
silence,
bring an end,
threaten the voice
and to cancel the self

it has no exit
it has no escape

its place in the mire
the bottom scum holds
bereft of illusions
devoid of those tools
that once gave flight fancy
that once loosened free
far along
gone away
down the path of no returns

2
the dirge rings within
        hope has died
        love has died

the dirge fills the air
        all is black mourning
        all is pyre ash

the dirge slows the day
        no good in living
        no point in breath

the dirge rings beyond
        man is dead
        earth is dead

3
and in the hollow
of the soul
and in the empty
of the mind
and in the spirit's
chilling dark
    there echoes blankness
    there echoes void
    there forms an ending
    there forms a death
made senseless by the lash of day
unjustified by times of life

    this comes
    like freezing winds
    on summer nights,
    this grips
    like sudden distance
    dropped away,
    this twists
    like facing unexpected loss
    and dying, rotting, exiled souls

it lies
in all things lies
all unprepared against expanse
and sightless
forced upon these dreams

ART IS TAKEN WITH THE NIGHT

the video invasion
motors apace:
    hard lines
    scan violent,
    naked,
    strange against
    the eerie glow

madness envisions this,
it reaches into darkness
and aligns against the sky

we are these:
    the sorry siltings
    of time alone,
    the ragged leavings
    of broken dreams
we eliminate:
    the foretaste of the winter,
    the shattered crystal end of time

despite all reason
hours take,
obtain their full decreeing span
and drop the veil of old deceit
    it is the agelessness,
    the whole course of the night

there is confusion here,
all elapses and is gone,
borders fall away in dreams
eradicating simple ways of past

extension programs,
illuminating the hidden:
    that is ransom
    that is unknowing
    small darks coddle
    the absence that is sight
lower is silence
the beat that clads the shine

DAYS REENACTED, STRUCTURED, FIT

the past is Nazca,
it bullies with
lines too true;
the fading grey lies
long on moonscape,
almost Mars,
almost too unlike
the Earth
so alien a place of stone
broken into dust

towards there
the cycles run return,
one of request,
not wishing made;
a dread hangs pregnant
in its shade,
its shadow hanging on for miles
with aftershocks
like shifting weight
around the necks of drowning men
not caring which
leads to the deep

pictures total up these coins,
make additions to the toll
compounding what has gone before;
an ocean bled out,
drop by drop,
not turned to gore
but rotting wet,
putrescence pulling in this tide

these corners spread,
become the night,
envelop all that wish to hide
with cloaks of fading,
capes of time,
sweet amnesia of the sun
so far away
as though in dreams
as though forgotten
despite the distance
held beyond

THESE DISTANCE THINGS, A JOURNAL

1
the place
exudes an idle waste
languid in its darkness,
frantic through eternal night

2
layers are placed
on top of layers,
shiftings incur
strange turbulence there

3
overfilling comes again
stripped of reason;
the maelstrom erupts
livid, pale,
and makes screams
for a retreat

4
stuck in mind like song,
gone by night like wind,
this is thematic
of extension towards the dark,
emblematic
of lateness and the hour

5
these questions run
from day to night,
their essence precludes sleep
and opens time
like hours stretched wide
in vistas too long,
a journey too lengthy
to allow for life

6
it falls out
from here,
it empties and is void
shattering the flow
of certainty,
breaking down
the will of play

7
again there is strangeness,
a juxtaposition
hanging two extremes
in sited light
so that the shadows
might play within the mind
strange puppet acts
with morality as theme

8
awaiting time with cash
eliminates duration's weight
yet defines itself
in terms of pressing,
in manners of expense

9
oh, dreams,
oh, great unsubtle
grinding dreams,
pulsing with the beat of life,
flashing in the patterned dark,
I long to reach
and touch your flesh,
to pump the sweat
hard through your night,
illusive
and so far off

10
the last
remains a transit thing
while sleep is coddled
high above the clouds,
rocked by movement,
the speeding shimmy
of our haste
still pressing on
to waiting morns

WORLD SHATTERED, SO FAR AWAY

what's the truth to this one?
your deities have no real names,
just hand-me-downs from other tribes,
later takers of this land,
their intonation
will not shake this valley
will not bring new breath to stone
convenient names
have little sway
when attributions are all false
and backwardsness portends decay

too many years have abused
this grid of streets laid out
in arcane angles,
unspoken pointings at old stars
now not with us
faded from the pantheon
of all the glimmering nighttime sky

synchronistic through these days
of heat and chill
power sought and commerce
denied, delayed,
all breaks apart
fear comes crystal in the light
of lying dogs bloodied and dead
as for a sacrifice to calm
invoking safety,
defusing night

words
misunderstood
in form
collapse the moment to one doubt
and leave a lingered sense
of subtle shiftings,
movement in the wind of time
which curls and eddies
in retro flows
to rip dimension,
overlay the strains of life

IN NIGHTMARES' SEED AND VISION'S EYE

you're buried there
I know
I walk round your coffin
and pry against the rotting boards
seeking to release some light
on the rottenness within
your symbols here abound
scattered like forgotten shells
amid the streams of busy life
not seeing, blind,
within some other world they move
but you and I,
we know the darkness of this realm,
the ways that illness grips the mind
and makes us wisdom's
bastard child

too many days are gone away
the plan has ashes at its edge
and maggot trails
and drips of slime
you chuckle from your stony grave
as though some other play was wrought
in all these failings

I turn away and slip the lines
to blinder sunny peopled worlds
yet hear that laughter in my head
as ridiculing you remind
me of the hollowness of day
when spirit must be sure to hide
beneath the shadow
within the grave
behind the glare of maddened eyes
that flail for mercy
but are given life

OF NAMES BECOMING PAST

death
breaks into life
and changes
things
alters
what we thought
was true
adjusts
the flowing of
our days
and makes anew
the vision
of who
and what we are

sadness creeps
into corners
filling gaps
left
in the fleeing haste
of time
seeping
through the seams
in being
filling out
perspective
without reason
without mind's assent

day
is darkened
pasts
are now defined
a sword has riven
through the night
cutting off
what was
from what will be
splitting
our history
from us
dividing
like chapters cracking
at ancient spines
into dust
apart

TORN INTO BRUTAL REALMS OF DEATH

1
battered by
conceptual space
in league
with sleep
conflicting
dimensional frames
erupt
killing clocks

2
tear out
the insides
of this night
eviscerate
the content
of these times
    I am damned
    within their course
    I am destined
    to pain's duration
    in these concepts' wake

3
terror is key
to any action
dread is script
to breath and life
I want to hide
to be away
I seek escape
a waking from these nightmares here
disguised as life
cloaked in masquerades of truth
that are like death
that bear the curse of poisoned race
against the screaming soul alone

ABOUT THESE POEMS

They say "may you live in interesting times" and mean it as a curse. The times that followed those represented in my previous book, "Into The Dark", fit this intent with sneering perfection.

As "Into The Dark" covered a period of years leading up to the onset of my sobriety, the current collection picks up after the long period of silence (nearly a year without doing any writing) that immediately ensued, and follows through the years 1986 and 1987. By 1987 I had resumed the pace of writing that I had attained in 1984 but had fallen away from amid the difficult intervening times, a level that is reflected in the distribution of the poems here, with about one third from 1986 and two thirds from 1987.

Again, these poems are arranged in chronological order, and were selected on a month-by-month basis to give an even feel to the flow of time. Hopefully there is movement here, hopefully life gets away from being "Amid These Empty Years".

- B.M.T.

www.ingramcontent.com/pod-product-compliance
Lightning Source LLC
Chambersburg PA
CBHW071741020426
42331CB00008B/2117